CW00869681

AN AFRICAN NAZARITE

AKIN IGE (PhD)

Copyright © 2025 Akin Ige

AMAZON PUBLISHERS

All rights reserved.

ISBN: 9798308566502

—

REFERENCES

The Holy Bible - all versions

DEDICATION

To YESHUA HAMASHIACH, my great Redeemer, who pulled me out of the mess of life and pushed me into prominence. I was not meant to live past seventeen, but my Redeemer has spared me for more than seventy years.

And to my immediate Family and extended family, and all who have contributed to my journey so far;

To all those who will read this story, which is my Epistle to the world, and would be transformed by the content.

ACKNOWLEDGMENTS

To my entire family, including my wife Fola, our children, and grandchildren, who have been the driving force behind my writing journey. Your support, feedback, and assistance in editing and designing the cover page have been invaluable.

I am deeply grateful to my dear friend, Pastor Professor Akin Bankole, for graciously writing the Foreword and for his insightful correction to the title of the book.

Special thanks to Dr. Mrs. Bola Agbaje for her thorough review and corrections of the earlier version of the manuscript.

To Folakemi Awe, my inlaw for her guidance in the publication

To all those who have influenced my life and work, igniting the fusion that has allowed my creativity to shine brightly.

To all the great people who have written excellent tributes in this book

To people - pastors and priests, professors and politicians- who put tremendous pressure on my wild grapes, that released the sweet wine, of purity and power.

CONTENTS

FOREWORD

It is a privilege for me to write a foreword for this divinely inspired and power packed biography of Professor Akinlolu Ige. I met the author about forty years ago, when we both started our academic career journeys at the then University of Ife (now Obafemi Awolowo University). Professor Ige rose through the ranks in the University and became a full Professor in earth sciences. This achievement is in acknowledgement of his incredibly successful research and amazing discoveries in his field of specialization. I also know Professor Ige as a giant of the Christian faith and a Priest of the Anglican Church, who equally rose through the leadership rank of his church. His successes as an academic and as a religious leader known and acknowledged worldwide are testimonies to the credibility and wisdom shared in this memoir. Professor Ige's unwavering faith underscores his belief in God's providence, manifested in miraculous deliverances from childhood perils and adult spiritual warfare, culminating in illustrious academic and religious careers. I therefore have no doubt that readers of the book are in for a treat.

My conviction stems not only from our shared academic and religious backgrounds but also from our common ethnic heritage in Nigeria, with parallel socio-cultural experiences. Professor Ige's personal anecdotes, mirroring my own struggles and triumphs against adversities, evoke the psalmist's words: "If it had not been the Lord who was on our side..." (Psalm 124:2-3,6). His narrative, replete with divine interventions and sagacious counsel, holds transformative potential for all.

The dichotomy delineated in the Bible between those reconciled to God through faith in Christ and those estranged due to self-righteousness forms the thematic nucleus of this book. For the first group, already anchored in faith, this book reaffirms their convictions, assuring them of God's abiding presence and protection.

Conversely, for the second group, it serves as a clarion call to embrace Christ's redemptive love and experience the transformative power of divine forgiveness. Jesus' invitation, "Come to Me, all you who labour and are heavy laden..." (Matthew 11:28-30), resonates throughout these pages, offering solace and salvation to the weary.

The Book offers its readers the love of God as well as the hope and assurance that come with giving one's life to God through Christ Jesus. As the Bible says, "Therefore, if anyone is in Christ, he is a new creation; old things have passed away; behold, all things have become new" (2 Corinthians 5:17). Given the evidential testimony contained in this book and the power of faith and hope in God it offers, I highly recommend it. One cannot overstate the life-changing impact of the book on those who would read it and by faith open their hearts to its counsels. Happy reading.

Akinrinola Bankole (PhD)
Lead Pastor, Abiding Love International Fellowship
Visiting Professor Ondo State Medical University, Nigeria

PREFACE

My motivation for writing this book is to testify that faith in God, through our Lord Jesus, works no matter what is happening in both the physical and spiritual world. Through the story of my triumph over defeat and overcoming human and spiritual obstacles, I aim to ignite success in others. I believe each success story will inspire countless individuals, spreading the doctrine that regardless of one's background, complexion, or the complexity of their circumstances, they can achieve unstoppable advancement towards prominence.

God, who created the universe, fashioned me in my mother's womb with His finest touch, rescued me from the clutches of the wicked, removed my filthy garment of sin, clothed me in the garment of salvation, and covered me with the robe of righteousness. He then commissioned me to proclaim His sovereignty over the universe He created. This book is the true story of how God's mercy lifted me from the depths of sin and failure, transformed my life, and empowered me to share His message with the world

To prepare myself for writing this book with compelling and creative evidence, God led me on a journey to numerous nations across the globe, starting in my own country before settling in the United States. I have had the privilege of interacting with diverse people and ethnic groups within my homeland and visiting dozens of cities on nearly every continent. I have spent countless hours interviewing individuals to grasp what drives achievement or impedes progress. Additionally, I have engaged with over six thousands students from kindergarten to college, as well as men and women in correctional facilities, sharing with them my experiences with God and the proven pathways to success that I have discovered.

From Lagos to London, from New York to New Delhi, in cities and in the suburbs of many nations in the world, I have concluded that kind and excellent people are present everywhere and that cantankerous people are not confined to any culture. The differences between the shining and dwarf stars are extremely thin: they are a product of insights and sufficient motivation that will kick start thermonuclear fusion that can push away the gravities of life!

As you read this book, billions of stars are being born by the breath of God, right from the divine nurseries. You can be one of those stars. Also, there are billions of failures being blasted off and being buried in the bottomless pit. The memory of those past potholes of life are also being erased, by the blotting blow in the blood of Jesus Christ. Through the mercies of God, the mistakes you made in every facet of life are headed for the bottomless sea of forgetfulness, deeper than the Mariana trench, where the demonic divers cannot dig; where the devious submersibles cannot descend into, and it is beyond the reach of satanic submarines!

I am inviting you to think about this incredible proclamation. No matter what has happened to you, no matter your level of degradation, God's mighty Potter's fingers can recreate you, refine you, regenerate and re-ignite your star. He can kick-start a thermonuclear fusion that will push away the gravity that is attempting to crush your life, to bring you out of all ashes of defeat, and cause your star to burn with a new bluish brilliance. You can succeed beyond all predictions and permutations of people around you. Please stay tuned!

To the struggling stars, I wish to state, that although your earthly resources have been messed up, there are heavenly resources still being created; a new nursery for stars is being formed from the death of your old stars! I have, therefore, come to say this to your life: Retrieve your life from the reverse or neutral gears: put it on drive gear, get up, jump up, get going, leave the rubbish of life and snatch back your stars!

INTRODUCTION
THE BEGINNING WORD- GOD LOVES YOU

I wish to state clearly from the beginning that I have nothing to boast about in life, other than the love of God that has soaked my life, His mercies that have rescued me from my disastrous adventures and His favors that surround me like a shield. It was the love of God and His mercies that brought me out of the mess of life and the miry clay of the world. I can identify with Paul when he wrote, 'Jesus Christ died for all sinners of whom I am chief!' I am what I am by the mercies of God, otherwise I would have died a miserable death long ago!

If you don't remember anything else in this book, it is very important to know that God loves you! He created you a masterpiece and put star genes in you that are waiting to be unleashed for your personal elevation, to solve some of the world's problems and more than anything else, to use you for His glory. God loves and thinks about you as clearly stated by an Old Testament saint David in Psalm 139. His thoughts are so merciful and many more than the sands of the seashore. They are infinite. They are more than the witness of man. With a grain of God's loving thought, you can ignore the negative comments of the entire people in all nations of the world.

The prosperity thoughts of God towards us are more powerful than the economic powers of the United States and all the NATO countries put together. His protection is more powerful than the nuclear warheads of Russia and all nuclear armed nations put together.

Think about our God, the creator of the universe, the owner of the sheep on a thousand hills, who created the stars and the galaxies and waters the earth from His chambers. Recently, astronomers found stars that are completely composed of pure diamond. And some current estimates put the numbers of such stars in their trillions.

The other gods are cold, they are distant, they are capricious cosmic nothingness! I have been privileged to confront many of these gods of the other nations on their soils. From the gods of the Yoruba in their cradles, to Buddha and Hindu, in China and India in their grotto, including their replicas in museums all over the world. They have no powers to do evil and it is not in their habits to do good.

When God created you from the dust, He used the Master Potter's creative fingers to deposit special genes into you. That is why your fingerprints are different from everyone else. God then puts you in some special assignments no one else can accomplish except you. When you try to fulfill this assignment by cutting corners, consuming drugs, and alcohol, you are corrupting your seed and giving the evil ones the ammunition to destroy you, and to make you belong to the dustbin of history. Under God, you have the power to stop the destiny derail and escape the black holes of life. I did that several years back, by connecting with the Creator, the Potter and preserver of mankind.

If you have failed before, you can rise from every ash of defeat. God has given me the grace to teach the subject of Astronomy for ten years, and to thousands of students across the continents of the world and one concept resonates with me: The death of stars creates nurseries for new stars and these new stars shine brighter than their older equivalent. We all (including the mightiest of men and women) have some stupid moments but you must never stay long in them because you don't belong there. Get up and hold on to the robe of righteousness in Christ Jesus and let us go together on a beautiful journey with the Master of the Oceans and the waves.

AN AFRICAN NAZARITE

CHAPTER 1
BRIEF BEGINNING OF MY PROGENITORS

I was born in a tiny village named *Shittu* on the Shasa riverbank about one hundred and forty miles southwest of Lagos, the commercial capital of Nigeria, West Africa. Both my parents have royal blood flowing through their veins. My Father was from the *Ikolaba* royal house of Modakeke while my mother came from the *Aaje* royal family in the same city. According to my father, his parents were of the Fakunle dynasty of the *Alagbaa Compound*, in Orile Owu, an ancient city, about forty miles west of Ile-Ife, the archaeologically famous cradle of the Yoruba civilization. Pa Fakunle gave birth to my father (Pa Daniel Ige and other female children. My great grandfather was known as Kilanko of the Ikolaba ruling house. He also gave birth to Ojo and other female children.

My father was an Owu immigrant to Modakeke. He was asked to move to Aregbe by his Aunt Mama Jekayinfa when his father died. She was a privileged woman, the wife of the Baale of Aregbe village, and possessed a strong and forceful character. It's unclear why my father initially settled in a village called Shittu by the Shasha River. Shittu was nearly decimated by a smallpox outbreak, and my family was one of only three to survive the epidemic.

Eventually, my parents moved to Aregbe village, where my father became a prosperous farmer and cocoa merchant, lending to other farmers in the village and beyond. His aunt played a significant role in helping him acquire extensive farmland, including the plot where he built a lovely home.

As a successful cocoa merchant, my father was known for his generosity and willingness to lend. However, when his mentor and the village head passed away, some villagers saw this as an opportunity to undermine my father. Cocoa farmers began to backtrack on their commitments to supply him with cocoa in exchange for the money they had borrowed. I vividly remember one particular instance when my father insisted on being repaid. One farmer retorted, "You are an immigrant here. Before you force me to pay, you must remove your house from our land." My father shed tears at this insult.

My father was gorgeous in dressing and great in generosity. He was a very religious and prudent man, with witty words. He walked majestically and shouted with authority; you could hear his commands from afar off, barking orders and laughing with all people. My father was exceptionally gifted with an excellent spirit, very wise and although he did not have formal western education, he was brilliant. He wrote perfectly in his native language and spoke some basic English which he picked up from the Adult Education classes he attended.

He was an only son of a very wealthy father and had opulence bestowed on him. From the story I heard from my mother, it appears he married at a very young age, perhaps younger than his wife. The background tends to corroborate this; he was an only son of a wealthy Owu man. Apparently, his father was urging him to get married.

He was loving to a fault and wielded great power in his prayers. A formidable intercessor, he faithfully led the local church in morning prayers for several years, making significant contributions to the growth of both the church and the community. Perhaps most significantly, his prophetic words spoken over my life continue to reverberate and guide me to this day.

No one is perfect and that included my father. He was a businessman but not shrewd or careful in handling money. His grandstanding with money led him to an early bankruptcy such that I could not go to high school for three years. He wanted me to inherit the farm he labored on and loved but my insistence on getting educated led to his having to go for brutal borrowing. To his credit he did not leave us with any debt to pay. His grave is standing as a polished marble within the Modakeke Anglican Cemetery till today.

My mother was a great intercessor too, a 'pristine' prophetess with an incredible force of optimism flowing through her veins. She was a great storyteller, and I probably inherited this skill. She was a great fighter when it came to protecting her children. Although she was afflicted with a mysterious sickness at the early stage of her marriage, she lived for more than ninety years, without gray hairs. Her eyes did not grow dim and her natural energy did not abate. Her grave is also standing strong with solid polished marble very close to my father's.

CHAPTER 2
THE VILLAGE VICTIMS AND THE VICTORS

As mentioned earlier, I was born in a small village situated on the banks of the Shassa River, approximately five miles west of Ile-Ife, the archaeologically renowned cradle of the Yoruba civilization in Nigeria. Sadly, the inhabitants of this village were devastated by a smallpox epidemic, and my parents were among the fortunate survivors

In those days, extreme poverty enveloped my surroundings. To grasp the depth of destitution in our village, envision a day spent in the bush, hunting rats just to secure a semblance of animal protein for our meals. Before a hunter could even contemplate taking down a deer or any sizable game, mastery of the craft was essential, accompanied by offerings to the god of the hunt; failure meant returning home empty-handed, famished, and embittered. Chicken or beef was a luxury reserved solely for rare occasions like church harvests or the New Year festivities. During avian outbreaks, the decaying remnants of chickens were our meager sustenance, freely bestowed upon us. Today, deer and squirrels roam freely around me, unchallenged, in stark contrast to my current abode in the United States.

Our toilets were conducted in open fields, our toilets mere pits amidst dunghills. You have to do it quickly, lest disease-ridden flies, resembling butterflies in size, descend upon one's excrement in a macabre feast, daring even to alight upon one's lips for a taste!

Shortly after my primary education, financial tragedy struck our home when my father lost his fortune to debt defaulters. That was in part the result of my father's indiscretion in loaning money to those who did not have the capacity to pay and what I regard as financial recklessness and monetary 'grandstanding'. That year, it appeared that the farmers held a "mutinous conference" and decided not to reimburse the cocoa merchants and as a result my father experienced a severe financial loss.

My father wanted me to inherit his very prosperous farmland; unknown to him, I had made up my mind to go to be properly educated and to excel. He inadvertently ignited this passion in me when he entertained the elites in our village. Once a year, my father made great feasts for them while I watched. As a young child, I looked at their form fitted shoes, their cherubic smiles and their gorgeous appearances and was enthralled. I vowed to be like them.

When my father lost his money to debt defaulters, and I couldn't go to high school, my emotion became negative. Because secondary education was not free at the time, the financial loss resulted in my inability to go on to attend secondary school immediately after primary school. Instead, I had to work as a subsistence farmer for three years. For my family, this was an ominous sign of bad luck because, as the first son, I was expected to be the breadwinner and the one who would uphold the dignity of the family name- and education was key. And in a desperate attempt to persuade my father to send me to school, I threatened that I was going into occultism; to become an enchanter so I can vanquish the forces that were withholding my breakthroughs. That threat jolted my father to action, and he had to borrow money to send me to school. He was forced to obtain a substantial loan, with 100 percent interest, to finance my secondary education when I could no longer be persuaded to stay on the farm.

That was how far my father was able to support my education. I would be forever grateful to my parents for this important step that served as a foundation for all my educational advancements. While I could not go to high school, I found myself immersed in the traditions of masquerades, akin to the veneration of the dead, reminiscent of Halloween festivities. For several years, I served as a temple lad at the shrine dedicated to the fearsome Oro, a deity within Yoruba mythology. Amidst the rituals of the occult, held in the shadowy recesses of clandestine meetings, I grew up amidst the stark realities of poverty, entrenched in the downtown alleys of destitution.

My days were plagued by the relentless torment of sicknesses. To secure a modest meal of 'amala'—a concoction crafted from mixed cassava flour—and abula, a soup made from assorted remnants, along with the toughened skin of Kwashiorkor-laden cattle, I toiled tirelessly, laboring under the scorching sun, sieving cassava flour for the local vendor.

Despite the allure of vice that surrounded me, with city dwellers enticing me towards indulgence in illicit activities such as promiscuity and smoking, my gaze remained steadfastly skyward. As I gazed upon the moon and the twinkling stars overhead, and watched the distant aircraft traverse the heavens, my aspirations to achieve greatness were reignited.

In that dreary and dark alley, in that disease laden, danger prone dungeon, God planted a daring dream in my heart. I dreamed I would succeed beyond all my progenitors put together. I saw my amniotic fluid being scattered by the strong arm of God, signifying I will travel to all parts of the word; I saw myself acquiring degrees upon degrees and living in an incredibly wealthy land. These dreams were later powered and propelled by the prayers of my parents, and my closeness to God, and I became unstoppable.

Although it took me several years of painstaking educational pursuits and many years of hard work in the best scientific laboratories in the world before I started to fly, God put power upon my dreams as a testimony of His rulership over the Universe. I still fly more than forty years later, eventually becoming a citizen of the United States and teaching wise, highly talented and regarded people all over the world. The breakthrough God has given me also included a very distinguished career as a full professor of geology and director of a foremost Natural History Museum in Nigeria. At the last count I have published more than 30 scientific articles, four literary books and have traveled to almost all the continents of the world.

CHAPTER 3
MY EARLY ENCOUNTERS WITH YAHWEH

I was born a Nazarite, dedicated to God Almighty from my mother's womb, but it took me more than sixty solid years of living, research, and study before I could unravel the mysteries of my birth and calling. I could recollect a cosmic event that occurred to me around the age of twelve years, when God appeared to me and put, as it were, a 'mark' on my forehead and an amazing dream in my heart. It was during my usual afternoon prayer time. I was sitting on my mat, singing from the Anglican Hymnbook and chanting the Psalms, when an amazing light shone around me. It was a cosmic event of gigantic proportion and has formed the basis of the greatness in my life. This invisible force was always driving me back to God, even without anyone witnessing to me. Later in life, I encountered the Lord Jesus Christ, gave my entire life to Him, received the baptism of the Holy Spirit, and today my dreams have swallowed up the dreams of the enemy.

I also remember a captivating myth that one of the elders in our village used to share with us during our nightly storytelling sessions. One such tale recounted his belief in how God intricately crafted the destinies of men and women. There was one story that left a lasting impression on me. He described how God would gather the amniotic fluid of each individual and scatter it from His celestial bedchamber; wherever this fluid touched the earth, the person to whom it belonged would inevitably reach that place before their life's end.

Right there, in the village with darkness around us, with dead destinies surrounding me, I caught and created my dream. I imagined that when God created me, He put into me star studded genes and then put me in the most obscure place on the planet. I imagined my amniotic fluid flying and scattering all over the world as God threw it with His outstretched hands!

The most interesting aspect of my life was that all materials needed to be famous were round about our house. God prepared those things for me before my forefathers were created. Our house is called *Ile olokuta* meaning the house on a rock. Those stones will eventually become the analytical materials for my PhD thesis. And it was in this same area that I discovered the ancient technologies of the Yoruba, which prompted a series of research that propelled me to prominence.

As a sign of a special person that was carrying a divine power, certain phenomena started showing up in my life. As a child, I was attacked by a deadly viral disease and I survived it: I drank poison and revived, was bitten by a charmed snake and my body vomited the venom. After surviving childhood satanic tornadoes, God gave me unusual physical strength, an incredibly sharp mind and a spiritual sense that surpasses common understanding. Moreover, he installed a bit of divine communicating spirit in me. In those days, I boasted about my dreams. Like Joseph, I had told everyone who cared to listen, that I was going to have university education; that I was going to be very great. I would summon my mates to read the great newspapers of that time to them, to propound great ideas, and to let them know the list of the white man's lands I will visit, presenting myself as a potentially famous journalist or scientist or a business baron. I told them of the nations I will visit and the number of PhDs I will acquire in science and arts. Then trouble began.

WHO IS A NAZARITE?

I started research on the Biblical Nazarite and found that several variants existed in the Old Testament times and must be in the days after Pentecost, and even now. There was a priest in Samuel, a soldier in Samson, a preacher in John the Baptist and a writer and miracle worker in the apostle Paul. Our Lord Jesus Christ is the Creator of all and all in all.

Nazarites are mysterious people that dramatically show up occasionally in a generation; as giant stars burning their spiritual fuels with incredible energies. They are imbued with the amazing insights, excellent skills and 'monster size' proportion of God's Shekinah. Most Nazarites are daredevil adventurers and many ended up committing blunders in the display of 'absolute power'. Many were power drunk, deploying spiritual energies with reckless abandon and some were very stubborn and impulsive people. Almost all of them were in running battles with the authorities at that time. They were also on constant combat operations against spiritual forces. That was perhaps the reason for putting a trailing and thorny demon on the heels of Paul the apostle (an episodic Nazarene), less he be exalted above measure. Elijah and his incarnated fellow and faith traveler, John the Baptist, were preachers and both went to heaven in a hurry.

Let us explore the case of the apostle Paul further. Paul was a power packed person even before he was converted. This incredible energy was a mechanical and spiritual disadvantage, until God smote him with blindness, took him on a spiritual retreat in the Arabian desert where his negative energy was converted to spiritual prowess for the glory of God. Then he became a real learned man in accordance with the law of grace and a repository of spiritual revelation, which led to the writing of most of the expository books of the New Testament. He also became a powerhouse for God, carrying tremendous unction, so that 'aprons and handkerchiefs' from his body carried powers to heal and to deliver.

We are not certain of the length of Paul's Nazarene vows and separation to God. Perhaps he took a vow during his fourteen silent years in the wilderness; but there was no doubt he took some episodic vows as recorded in Acts of the Apostles, Chapter 21. But he had great deals of angelic visitation, perhaps more than the other apostles. He was a first-class evangelist and spiritual giant burning spiritual energies with incredible 'thermonuclear fusion'. He was also a very stubborn stick-necked adventurer!

Imagine what would have been the story of Paul, if he heeded the warnings of the Holy Ghost through prophetic words which went before him. Even the hands-on demonstrations and display to show impending danger by eminent prophets like Agabus; and the virgin prophetesses, in the house Philip could not dissuade the wayfaring man of God. Was the rugged apostle looking to be a martyr for Jesus or was he grandstanding by willing to shed his blood as an atonement for what he had done in the past; a serial sin that was paid for in full by Christ? Or was he plain tired of life and wanted to stampede the return of our Lord? These are open questions for you and I to ponder upon.

Samson was a spiritually stupid Nazarites who had an unclean demon hanging on his genitals! I believe he would have fared better if he had parents who were profound and persistent intercessors. But instead of Samson's parents going on prayers and fasting for him, they let him loose and did his careless reckless bidding. Perhaps he would have been spared the marriage to the strange occult woman and would not have lost his eyes and dignity. His case was like Paul's in some respects. He was full of energy but fell into the hands of his vicious enemies. After losing his eyes and being brought low and was grinding mill, God again had mercy on him, and restored his strength. His hair-lock, the sign of his separation as a Nazarite, began to grow. Then he prayed to God to kill him, together with his enemies! If I were Samson, I would ask God to open my eyes, as he has restored my hair-locks. Then Samson could still have conquered his enemies and delivered the whole of Israel from this vicious Philistine army. He could have become another testimony of physical and spiritual restoration from our loving God.

But he chose death rather than life. That is what happens to a man who has lost power and has been confined to a small space, to recuperate and be restored. But he could have won a landslide victory for Israel and Judah, such that even the mention of his name could have sent shivers to the spines of the Philistines, hundreds of years after he had gone to rest!

Why did Paul and Samson go to heaven in a hurry? Why did they stampede heaven to take them up? Depression! They had accomplished so much and won many battles that they thought their time was up. They felt abandoned and irrelevant to the powerhouse at Jerusalem. Left out of the scheme of things, without family and close friends, they could not endure their personal Patmos. This is perhaps because there were no smart communication gadgets to monitor the situation in Jerusalem. And the elders, less educated and less successful were calling the shots at home. That is my interpretation because I felt this way too when I had to start life again in a strange land after accomplishing so much in Nigeria.

Although I have experienced almost all the blunders of the Nazarites, God Almighty caused me to escape them all. I was on a rampage for Christ and on the run from people, but God has shown mercy on me, by taking me on a new journey in life, stripping me of earthly power and politics; and causing my 'hair locks' to grow again.

CHAPTER 4
THE NAZARITE IN ME

God has enabled me to live an extremely mysterious life from my youth. Anywhere I appear, something great will happen to change the destinies of those homes, those communities and churches, cities or even nations. I had a very difficult life and there is no doubt that an invisible hand has been guiding and guarding me. Any object I touch becomes 'gold' and my research topics have become the bride of many famous laboratories in the world. God has given me grace to succeed beyond my equals, and in near impossible circumstances. My words are powerful, with the Holy Spirit 'laser guided precision'. Anyone who shows kindness to me soars; and anyone who attempts to cross my path is crushed by an invisible force. Also, I have escaped every dungeon dug by the devil and have survived several daredevil adventures and acts that were capable of crushing my destiny.

During my teenage years, I had a profound encounter with God, during which He installed several alarm clocks within me. These alarms served as warning signals, guiding me away from paths that could have led to detrimental consequences. Among them were alarms for sugar, alcohol, food, and spiritual matters. Notably, there was also a relationship alarm, which prevented me from entering into unions with individuals who did not align with my Nazarene creed and commitments, safeguarding my spiritual integrity. Whenever I veered close to transgressing these principles, these alarms acted as a firm reminder, jolting me back to reality and steering me back towards God. It's crucial for each of us to recognize and heed the alarms embedded within our own beings.

While they may differ from person to person, their ultimate purpose is to guide us toward Godliness and righteousness, ensuring we stay on the path of our destined journey.

It was when I finished teaching my college students who were incarcerated in jailhouses, and I was waiting to be 'discharged' from my classroom that God opened my understanding to why my life was running in this peculiar way. God opened my understanding to the fact that special children have difficult times, and I had my fair share of them. It took me almost sixty years of living to discover that I was dedicated to God from my mother's womb. I was an African Nazarite, who was conceived after my mother had dared and defied the most powerful wizards in south-western Nigeria.

According to my mother, who came from one of these African power houses, she secretly converted to Christianity through the guidance of her father, who strangely was an occult warlord, whose herbal prowess was second to none in that area of south-western Nigeria. They were descendants of the priests of the dreaded Oro, the furious vengeful god of the Yoruba. No notable medicine man, spiritual malefactor or the dreaded masquerades could operate without the annual obeisance call at our family house. That person will walk naked and as the saying goes, 'eat his pounded yam as raw yams'.

That same man, the head of the herbalists and a chief priest who was my maternal grandfather, quietly coached his children in the Anglican Catechism and allowed them to be baptized into the Anglican Church. The reason for doing that is an open question. Did he know something that others did not know? Could he have been a version of the priest of the Midianites, Moses' father-in- law who impacted both the spiritual and administrative lives of Moses? Or was he in the mould of Balaam, another priest from that part of the world? Such people had revelations of God, which were distorted by idolatry. Or maybe my grandfather was just interested in adding Christian power to his native signet.

My mother with her pristine purity, and primitive faith went on rampage with her faith in God, by bulldozing her way to marital prosperity. When she got married to my father, another covert from a priestly home, who himself was a great man of faith, she immersed herself in the church's tradition of daily prayers and weekly fasting. Her faith was however tested when she had three female children one after the other, which was considered an affront to my father's masculinity and an ominous signal the lineage was about to be terminated. In many cultures in those days, you were a failure if you didn't have a male child to perpetuate your father's name. Men in such a position became desperate, and either took more wives or became 'sexually out of control' donating their spermatozoa indiscriminately, producing free range children who may eventually turn out to become vagabonds!

The fourth pregnancy which produced me triggered a spiritual tornado. While I was in the womb, my mother was summoned by the ancient medicine men to take a 'male hormone', a concoction that would have automatically changed my sex from female to male. Apparently their 'spiritual radar' could not locate me, and their diagnostic machine could not determine my sex because I am a special person, of a higher spiritual rank. My mother refused and dared the wizards with her simple primitive faith. Because of the daredevil action of my mother, those devious people were waiting on the wings, to unleash vociferous vengeance once I appeared on planet earth. That was probably one of the reasons for all my troubles – and my mouth! But thanks be to God, who makes me ride on his powerful wings.

According to my mother, my birth was like a time of celebration for the arrival of an avatar into the world. That night, 'the king of the compound' (my father) could not sleep because of the impending birth of a fourth child during a ravaging smallpox outbreak in our village. I was an 'ultimatum' child, a matching order for my mother to give birth to a baby boy or risk her position and possession in the family. Since there were no diagnostic machines that could determine the sex of the baby, everyone waited with bated breath for my arrival.

As earlier stated, my mother had (for some strange reason) refused to yield to pressures that she took some concoctions that would have ensured that I was born male, and therefore was preparing a suicidal showdown with the herbalists and ancient medicine men. To further complicate the issue on my birth, I was going to come out as a breach and a potential mother 'murderer'. When I was born male, my father was jubilant; he took off the best of his clothes, the 'aran' (damask) and rapped me as a most precious child. From there my troubles began.

CHAPTER 5
A NAZARITE POWERED BY MY PARENTS' PRAYERS

Unlike most Nazarenes I read about, my parents' prayers were pivotal to my achievements. Those powerful prayers preserved my life from irreversible errors, protected me from the clutches of the wicked people and unleashed in me the power to dream creatively.

Perhaps Samson's story could have turned out differently if his parents prayed for him as my parents did. But they gave him only tepid protests at his outlandish behavior and his out-of-control sexual adventures. Not me. My father pounded me with canes until the devil in me was overthrown; and then prayed the artifacts of the renegade behaviors out of their hiding places in my belly. The result: I never smoked, never joined any evil gang, never became a drunkard and all attempts to marry strange women collapsed like a pack of cards!

My father never went to school but exposed me to three important levers to success: godliness, hard work and prayers. My parents pumped progress and prosperity into my life despite the painful punishing words I was exposed to in the world. No one gave me a chance to succeed; the enemy unleashed the most potent forces and fury against my destiny. Everyone, old and young, colleagues and friends thought that I was a wrong child and will never amount to anything. All I heard from the time I could hear clearly, was negative. From people to priests, from teachers to colleagues, it was: "You will forget this." "You don't have a good voice." "You are not a gifted child'. "You are a 'Sickler'.

No one gave me a chance except my parents and grandmother. First, my parents gave me two great names- Olugbenga (God makes me great) Akinlolu (God is a valiant warrior). Although I was afflicted with diseases, sicknesses, and some crash failures, God has used me to break family and economic jinxes, and even national laws have been changed to favor me!

My father's blessing had landed on my forehead and had carved for me a colorful destiny before people came forth to try and plant darts and dirt of negative words into my life. He woke me up every day to pronounce blessings on me before he left for early morning prayers in our village church, one and a half miles away. I believe he must have continued the invocation all through his routines, because of the enemy that was rampaging and ripping through youthful lives, consuming them with fury and fangs. My father would come back to find me still sleeping and would liberally pronounce blessings on me again on arrival. So, before the mountains were brought forth, before my enemies could identify me in the crowd, my parents had cooked me in the pot soup of prayer 'concoctions'.

Before my haters were born, I have been blessed by those who mattered. I then went ahead to connect with the source of supernatural blessing by being washed in the blood of Jesus Christ. This made my parental blessings irreversible. What killed other children could not kill me and what afflicted other children could not harass my destiny. I was attacked by all manner of plagues, smallpox, and yellow fever. My body was at a time, a locus of tapeworms but I survived them all. So, when the other diseases showed up in the world, the unexplainable super immunity of God prevailed!

I don't remember some of the words of my father's blessings now but they have made inroads for me everywhere in the world. They made the slightest efforts to bring forth unexplainable success. They kept me from being a drunkard, getting involved with strange women and from smoking cigarettes or dope and they propelled me into conversion.

Here is a graphic illustration of parental power of pronouncements that will excite your faith: I was taking the finals of my high school diploma examination when I collapsed in the classroom. In those days, the diploma was a meal ticket and getting it gave people a gateway to jobs in the civil service, in the teaching profession and countless company jobs. Many parents sold even their last possessions to send their children to high school. This act, in many instances, guaranteed sweet returns for parental labor and would take that family name to the limelight. The graduate became a breadwinner, a light bearer, and a financial sponsor for the siblings. My father had taken a substantial loan, with a very high interest rate to get me this far. Here was I, dying from some mysterious disease.

The hospital could not determine the cause of my sickness and therefore discharged me home to die. I was almost losing consciousness on my sick bed at home when I noticed the most powerful herbalist in our city enter the room. He had been summoned in an emergency (African version of 911), because many other young men and women had died in similar circumstances and my parents wanted me to live at all costs. This man was noted for summoning the spirits of the dead, famous for being a competent intercession on behalf of victims of witchcraft and was a celebrated master-dealmaker when it concerns appeasing witches and familiar spirits. With my half-closed eyes, I saw his frightened face and heard his heavy sigh. His diagnosis, which made my father weep profusely, was on my impending, certain death!

This was a time of special satanic upheaval in our village when the witches went out of control. They overthrew their husbands who were renowned witch doctors, cursed the herbs, made the special concoctions impotent and destroyed the powers of the enchanters, the diviners, and the conjurers. The aged herbal veterans among the men, in panic, went out of the area to obtain extra powers from the gods of another land where the witches could not dare to invade. Coming back, they were thoroughly beaten again, and their sorrows became 'buy one, get one free'. The witches seized the moment, devoured both young and old, and even spread their evil tentacles to those who fled into exile. There was weeping and gnashing of teeth everywhere in the land, as death loomed large on every home and hamlet in the land.

It was during this terrible moment that I was struck down with an unknown disease, right at the very edge of my breakthrough. The gods were angry as usual and had demanded to drink the warm blood of another brilliant, promising young person. By this time, I was already eating the bread of the dead; I was already passing to the other side. As the master witch doctor stepped out of the house in resignation, my grandmother, a veteran in her own version of spiritual warfare, came in. It appeared she was making a last effort to 'persuade' me to stay alive. I could not hear what she said clearly, but I faintly heard something about my dream; something like this: '...Akin don't die with your dreams'.

In those days, I boasted about my dreams. Like Joseph, I had told everyone who cared to listen, that I was going to have a university education; that I was going to be very great. I would summon my mates to read the great newspapers of that time to them, to propound great ideas, and to let them know the list of the white man's land I will visit, presenting myself as a potentially famous journalist or scientist or a business baron. I told them of the nations I will visit and the number of PhDs I will acquire in science and arts.

Then I remembered one of the elders in the village used to tell us night stories and myths. One night he told us how he thought God created men with destinies. There was a particular story that stuck with me. He said God will normally take the amniotic fluid belonging to each person and scatter it right from His bedchamber in heaven; wherever that person's amniotic fluid touches ground, he/she will certainly get there before he or she dies. Right there, in the village with darkness around us, with dead destinies surrounding me, I caught and created my dream.

I imagined my amniotic fluid flying and scattering all over the world as God threw it with His outstretched hands!

My dream! As soon as my grandmother reminded me of my dream, my spirit revived. I woke up to taste food I could not touch for four days. I was totally healed, completed my high school and went ahead to fulfill my dreams. There is an explosive power loaded in parental pronouncements especially when they know the Lord Jesus and are bolstered and guided by the words of His power. When you are baptized in the Holy Ghost, you become unstoppable! Satan is too small to smash your destiny, because the templates have been 'figured out' with the very fingers of God.

Israel was delivered from the Egyptian trenches by the voice of the prophets; they went through the wilderness, crossed the Red Sea and Jordan, defeated their enemies and it is still a great nation today, by the voice of prophecy. I went through my own version of exodus, by the word of prophecy. Because of the words that have gone ahead of me, and my personal commitment to Christ Jesus, God has made all things succeed in my hands! In my academic adventures, I have got funding and financing for all my research from all world organizations, traveled to almost all parts of the world free, and eventually became a citizen of the most advanced and wealthiest nation in the world.

I am always aware that some forces follow me everywhere to get me things I was not even entitled to. Whenever I touch anything: church matters, scientific matters, family matters, they succeed automatically by the powers of the Holy Spirit. For example, the Lord God gave me grace to be appointed as Director of an institute at the university. Before I came to the headship of the institute, it had become an albatross, a failed scientific estate. The building designed for it lay moribund for over twenty years before God brought me to the scene to complete an architectural masterpiece, which is still the talk of the museum world until today. If you discover what I discovered, you can never get stuck again.

Each time the enemy rose to swallow me in his usual fury, these words that God put in the mouth of my father, raised standards against him. What killed other children could not kill me and what afflicted other children could not harass my destiny. I was attacked by all manner of plagues, such as smallpox and yellow fever. My body was at a time, an epicenter for tapeworms and a pillar of disease germs. I was afflicted by bowel, bone, and blood diseases but God has made me come forth as gold, flushed feebleness from my life, gave me life in its fullness and then gave me this mandate to use for His glory.

That is the message I am introducing here in this book. Jesus Christ, the master of the oceans and the waves, who rolled away the stones at resurrection of Lazarus and himself, and sat on it, will make you an overcomer. Amen

In every battle that our children are going through, in all satanic flares that are affecting them and in all their struggles, we have a say, even the answer. It is in our mouths. Satan cannot stop us, demons cannot make demands on us, and the wicked cannot waylay us. It is our God ordained duty, backed by His signet of power, enforced by the hosts of heaven, and unstoppable by the forces from the pit of hell. We even stand on a better ground when we belong to Christ, are blood washed and living our lives in obedience to the word of God.

CHAPTER 6
SOME MORE SECRETS BEHIND THE STORY

When God took me out of my mother's womb, the village vultures flew over me to crush me with all manners of childhood diseases and cataclysmic events. The demons came out of their dens to attempt to devour my life. The forces of evil gathered to attempt to distort my destiny or at least to confine me into a corner, as a dwarf star without enough thermonuclear fusion, which is necessary to shine as a full star. However, God loaded me with extreme brilliance and masked it with a deep black brilliant and beautiful skin, so I could spring surprises on those who take me for granted. He gave an incredibly sharp mind that I still remember what happened when I was a toddler. Most people I have encountered in my life's journey always thought I needed their help when they saw me, until I brought out the spiritual springs on my feet and most people thought I was a push over until I displayed the fighting claws on my fingers!

And God stood stoutly behind me as smallpox ravaged my village of birth, to show the world His own could survive any storms. Then He guided my parents to flee with me to a village which was noted for witchcraft, where the land drank the warm blood of young men and women. He watched over me as I grew up when a financial disaster struck my family so I couldn't go to school. During those times of inertia, He watched over me as hemp and cigarette smoking youth tried to influence me, when the occult tried to recruit me and when diseases smote me.

I am writing this book to people who are struggling all over the world. I have been in such struggles myself and it was worse. I was raised in a village where you must spend a whole day in the bush hunting for rats before you could eat meals containing decent proteins. Before the hunters could kill a deer or other big game, he had to be a veteran shooter and had to make sacrifices to the god of the hunting, otherwise he would come back home empty handed. Today, those same deer and squirrels walk around me unchallenged.

Dare to dream great dreams and get your hand stuck into the everlasting arms of the Almighty God, and He will fish you out!

When I was born as a Nazarene, there was an alarm in the camp of the wicked, that an avatar had arrived and the only one option available was to make me 'a still-born dwarf star'. There was a daylight display of negative energies to crush the star gene in me and thereby consigning me to the dustbin of history. That was why I had to fight both physical and spiritual billows, most of my life to push back all these negative energies. But the Lord God who separated me from my mother's womb, smashed the fingers that were waylaying me, and destroyed all destiny manipulators who were attempting to crush my life.

However, it took me more than sixty years to realize I was an African Nazarene. My mother gave me some hints earlier in life and my uncle confirmed that I was an 'obi funfun' uncommon among the Kola Nuts because it is impossible to plant them, they just pop up. My mother did not have a complete understanding of what she did (or she was not eloquent enough to describe it). But as soon as I survived my childhood sickness episodes, she urged me to join the choir of my church and took me to certain prophets to enquire about my future. I remember this particular prophetess who compared my life to a powerful governor of a region of my country; that is, if I ever made it to adult life!

My mother and I were constant faces at the Pentecostal revivals in those days, sipping blessed waters, swallowing anointing oil, and mimicking speaking in tongues, with sincerity and zeal. It was a matter of life or death, and I was determined to live, despite my disease-ridden body, and the presence of powerful people who were prepared to swallow me up.

Several times (as an adult) I had this urge from the Spirit of God to take episodic vows by allowing my hair to grow for prayer purposes especially during my many research trips abroad. Such times were times of unusual power surge and incredible successes spells.

CHAPTER 7
HOW I SOARED ABOVE MY SCARS

My whole body is full of scars, scary scars. The largest of them is on my left thigh. And my mother told me the story of that scar. It was caused by a fire accident when I was a baby. A wood fire, meant to warm my small body, crossed its boundaries and burned me. This wound could have triggered a tetanus infection that might have led to an early grave. I have another large one between my eyes that could have blinded me in one eye. There were many other scars! Not only that, but there were also emotional scars.

Scars are symptoms of unfairness in the physical and emotional worlds. It came into the world because of the intervention of the archangel Satan in the smooth relationship between God and man. That is the reason the Son of God our Lord Jesus Christ was manifested, that He might restore our scarred destinies to smooth beautiful brilliance designed since the beginning of our birth.

God's very powerful hands that brought me out of my mother's womb have made me to soar above all my scars. Through His mercies, I have become many times better than all my progenitors and peers and I have succeeded beyond the predictions of people and prophets. Satan is a scar monger, but our God is a scar mender!

What lesson can we learn from our scars? The moon is full of scars and craters created by the pelting of an asteroid, and meteorites, yet you can sometimes read at night through the brilliance of its radiance. Why? Because it reflects the radiance of the sun. It leaves its imperfections and scars. So, we should leave our scars and radiate the glory of God.

The scars could not stop me from succeeding excellently, and it should not stop you. The powers of the Spirit of God that work in us is greater than the scars. You too can succeed. Yes, you can succeed beyond your own imaginations and the predictions of your peers! Although I didn't start well, I am bent on finishing well! And you too can. Yes, you can.

The greatest error in life is focussing on the scars, and clinging to memories we should be releasing, while forgetting the boundless goodness of God in an instant. Even scientific evidence reveals that negative memories often occupy more space in our minds. For instance, when fifty people commend you for a job well done and only one person offers a negative armchair criticism, it's typical to remember that single negative comment more vividly than the plethora of positive feedback.

Negative memories can flood our minds. Thankfully, we possess the power to change the channel, rather than passively sitting in front of a negative movie screen. David, referred to by God as a man after His own heart, never concluded his Psalms in despair. He did not entertain bad days.

We can thwart the enemy's advances by refusing to replay hurtful moments, wrong choices, or abusive scenarios. They are like scars with healing layers; attempting to pick at them only reopens the wounds. Let's cease aiding the devil in accusing our brethren. Instead, let's shift our focus to our achievements, spiritual victories, and cherish moments when God intervened in our lives.If you've made mistakes, be grateful for the chance to start anew. Stop being your own adversary.

The children of Israel were instructed to commemorate annual feasts as memorials to God's victories and blessings. What memorials are you establishing? Perhaps when you met your spouse, purchased your first car, welcomed your children, or answered a calling.

Have you faced rejection? So has Paul, the traveling apostle, endured rejection, imprisonment, and disruptions in his journey for Jesus Christ. Despite closed doors, new windows opened for him to minister and bear witness for the Master. All our forefathers of faith faced rejection, from Abraham to our Lord Jesus Christ. Paul's experience serves as a profound example. How did he combat rejection? By rejoicing.

I have encountered much rejection in my life, breeding frustration and bitterness. God had to physically remove my gallbladder, which had become a repository for my bitterness! The accumulation of stones in my gallbladder mirrored the buildup of bitterness due to rejection. Its removal freed me from the bile and bitterness I had harbored, stemming from a lifelong battle against rejection—a messenger of Satan, as Paul described it.

CHAPTER 8
THE MINISTERIAL STORMS

When the Lord God 'dragged' me into the ministry, He equipped me with an extraordinary physical drive and unique divine energy, causing alarm in the enemy's camp. He rescued me from the wilderness of life, the curse of underachievement, the clutches of witches and wizards, and from diseases and degradation. He then propelled me into the limelight, enabling me to preach everywhere, write books, and broadcast prayers on radio and TV.

God has been gracious to me. He used me to build renowned churches, adorn His cathedrals, and transform the lives of hundreds of young people who now hold significant positions in many nations. I am grateful for the congregations I pastored and the priests I worked with, as they all contributed to my achievements in the ministry.

There were, however, very scary storms, which are to be expected when confronting the forces of evil directly in deliverance crusades, outreaches, and prayer sessions. Yet, God showed mercy on me, took me out of the war front, renewed my ministerial mandates, and launched me into the limelight once again. Very few people have been so favored!

I was a 'commander' in a bloody spiritual war in southwestern Nigeria, in the very heart of idolatry, the so-called cradle of Yoruba civilization. I was a deliverance minister and went into it with my whole heart, and sometimes with far-right bulldog tenacity. I was referred to as a 'German Machine' of evangelism and prayers. And God has been gracious to me that the war did not consume me. For both ancient and contemporary warfare, most commanders of dare- devil missions either never survived or they had to go through a very long and painful reminiscence of war, and it may take years of therapy to recover from internal and external wounds. It has taken me almost ten years to fully recover from my wounds, but I did, through God's grace

The Christian journey is like a combat operation, especially if you ministered in the deliverance ministry, like I did. After each operation, you need to start a process of damage control, if you lived long enough for a thorough reflection. The enemy will try to come against you on the sea of life as he did for Paul in Acts 27 and 28; even your family may rise against you, but God is the restorer and the repairer of the broken pieces of life.

And God has shown some unique mercy on me, took me out of my country of birth, reversed 'my mortgage', put my life in neutral gear and now in high forward gear. He put new sharp neurons in my brain, new excellent spirit in my heart, new health in my body, and opened to me a vista of doors which no one could shut. But then God took me to a tiny 'solitary spiritual confinement'. I was removed from the noise, from the fame and from the fanfare. It was difficult and I was tempted to fight the confinement, until my eyes were opened to the benefits, and the blessing beckoning at me.

Why will God who has been so gracious to me all these years abandon me in old age; why will a benevolent God take me to several cities across the planet and then punish me with penury? When God brought me to the United States, I wanted to live a very simple churchman's life of teaching the word of God and God gave me great opportunities to preach at several churches, even beyond my state. However, the catastrophic spiritual convulsion within the church I was involved in pushed me to become an independent priest engaged in intercessory prayers, and back to my teaching career. But the storms could not stop my dream for the service of God. Under God, I now wear the priestly robe, with the priestly ephod and prophetic power.

The ministerial storm I went through was similar to the kind of storm experienced by Paul, the rugged apostle, on the high sea after surviving an assassination attempt in Jerusalem. The name of that storm was even more jaw- breaking. I think that Paul having caused a violent rupture in the kingdom of darkness, during his deliverance ministry and unceasing upheavals in the hierarchical kingdom of the Pharisees, because of his mutinous movement, was sent the most vicious storm by the combined forces of men and evil angels. They waited on the high seas to finish him!

If you read the story in Acts 27 and 28, you will find out that the most dangerous weapons of the devil were on display, to settle a long- term spiritual score with Paul. First, the devastation by the storm by ripping the ship apart, then the soldiers attempted to kill all prisoners, which would have included Paul, then the serpent came out of the heat, to attack the wayfaring apostle. But what happened dazed the devil and the enemies of Paul and dazzled his friends. When Paul was attacked by a viper that came out of the fire, they waited for him to die. When they saw that he was still standing, they concluded he was a god. I pray that you also will be perpetually victorious and be still standing on your feet, no matter the assaults from the pits of hell.

When the storm hit, the barbarians on the ship decided to try common sense. They freed themselves from excess baggage to lighten their burdens and prepare themselves for some divine intervention. Whether they consulted the oracles, or read the constellations, they were facing the reality that even if they were going to die, it must be worth it. They decided they could do without some items they once were sure they needed.

Christians carry monster size extra baggage that hinders the flow of grace and consigns the carrier to the unnecessary pressure cooker of conflicts. A great example is un-forgiveness, bitterness and of course envy. Bitterness is like drinking poison and hoping it will kill your enemy. And of our extra cargoes, may be bad things we have accumulated like barnacles: a compromising relationship, deepening debt, a growing obsession with money, an entangling sinful habit, critical attitude- things we hang on to until a storm exposes how they are sinking us. A storm is our chance to change. When the rough subsides, we can return to the same overloaded or wrongly loaded lifestyle. That in turn could set a stage for an even bigger storm. If you want to survive your personal hurricane, evaluate extra cargo and get rid of it – with your own hand- before it sinks you.

Dear friend, are the storms lashing at you and things that are yours? I wish to put it to you that you are stronger than the power of all storms, whether they emanate from natural or demonic sources. The storms cannot stop you. The soldiers cannot harass you and the serpents cannot molest your destiny. All the combined forces of darkness cannot be a match for the awesome, wonderworking, demon-shaking, miracle working power of our Lord Jesus; that is the power that works in us!

I remember the song we used to sing in those days – "with Jesus in the boat I can smile at the storm." It's now your turn to smile at that storm trying to ravage your life and trying to finish your marriage or ministry. You can also smile at the soldiers and disdain the serpent. All you need is for Jesus to be right in your boat every time, everywhere and not just a silent listener to your spurious or odious conversation! Let him know where you are, what you are doing and where next you are going. Then you will not only survive the storms, but you will also sail. Amen.

CHAPTER 9
THE POWER OF A POSITIVE FAMILY

My wife Fola was given to me by the inspiration of God, and I will forever praise Him for this amazing gift. And God has been merciful to us to keep our marriage strong and very successful. As I went on rampage against the occult, and preached from cities and villages, she was my spiritual backup. My wife is a great gift from God, a calming care for my boisterous emotions. She is the best cook, the best intercessor, and a submissive wife. To God be all the glory for keeping us alive together, healthy, and strong this day.

I could recollect when I first proposed my love to her more than forty-seven years ago, we were substitute teachers at a popular elementary school in Ile-Ife Nigeria. Through my pristine prophetic eyes, I saw in her a treasure that could not be tarnished, and a woman I could spend my life with. I saw her cherubic smile, her polished appearance, gentle voice, and your beautiful countenance. Although we were too young to embark on a marriage journey, and both of us went ahead to accomplish greater things for ourselves and encountered Jesus Christ at different times, Divine Providence brought us together six years later. Since we got married more than forty years ago, that treasure in her has never tarnished. She has been a diligent wife to me and a caring mother to our children. She performs her duties with unusual energies, with laser beam focus and with bulldog tenacity. We were never aware of food shortages, never afraid for the snowstorms, never lacked the oils on our heads and she has excelled above all women.

We have fought many battles of life together side by side, under God. We have spent our resources together, both to train our children and to care for us all. We have interceded together and ministered side by side under God. We have struggled and sailed together as companions and co laborers.

There are still many stories to tell about our testimonies of a very successful marriage. There are still many things to laugh about; so much love to share again, so many stories of God's faithfulness to tell our children and grandchildren. There are still many things to hope for and much faith to linger on, under God, because our marriage is still a work in progress… I pray for good health, and a sound mind to long enjoy the fruits of her labor.

In the training of children, we have enjoyed the mercies of God. We have learned from my childhood experience that the prayer of parents is the most potent force that can mold our children's destinies. I had a horrible beginning in life. But for my parents' prayers, I would have ended my life in the dustbin of history. There were too many negative forces that were waiting to punch destiny out of my life. There were cold and cantankerous people around me that were ready to crush my creativity, and to consign me to a corner of underachievement. But God was with me, and my parents cried to him daily and prophesied positive words on my life

We need to constantly pray for our children from childhood to old age. Instead of worrying and having sleepless nights on our children, let us hand their lives and destiny to the faithful all-knowing God. The prayer project on our children is not complete until we breathe our last breath on earth. If we stand on our watch as my parents stood for me, under God, nothing, and absolutely nothing can pluck our children from the gracious hands of God. If they honor God more, then they will even receive multiple of the power we carry and succeed beyond all their peers and all predictions. I even believe that when we join the saints triumphant in heaven, we can still join their intercessory 'group' to send prayers to our children on earth!

All our fathers of faith had some troubles raising children and we had our fair share, but God causes us to triumph in all issues of life. From the calamitous mistake of Abraham who acceded to raising a generation who now troubles the world with satanic teeth, to Isaac and Jacob they had tremendous troubles. For example, Jacob had Rueben who was sexually out of control, donating his 'electrons' everywhere, to Simeon, the instrument of cruelty and of course, Judah and his train of tragic children. Not to mention David or Eli or even Samuel.

The troubles are part of the satanic struggle for our heritage from God. Satan knows that children are our arrows of defense from God, and he is not willing for us to have our quivers full of them without a fight. He knows his time is short, therefore he wants to contend with the destiny of our children. But we have the sure and certain word of God for our children. God says He will 'contend with those who contend with us, and He will save our children'. He says all that 'our children will be righteous and great shall be their peace.' And that He will write His laws into their hearts. These words are perfect, they are powerful and can never be violated by the wicked ones, under our watch. We should stay as prayer combatants and crush the enemies of our children at the gate.

While we constantly intercede for our children, we should give them space to grow in the grace of God. We should surrender their destinies to their Creator God and not be 'surveyors' of our children. I learned this lesson the hard way, and I have watched 'movies' that played or are still playing in the lives of many parents struggling with this problem. For example, I have watched some parents die calamitous deaths because they were not ready to give their children breathing space. In the process, they confronted the God of Elijah and were consumed by fire. I have watched a well-meaning friend almost consumed by the terrible worries for children whom he was unwilling to release from his firm, emotional grips. If you love your children so much, why don't you leave them in the hands of the Creator of the Universe, the Moulder of all destinies and the controller of the very breath in our nostrils? Why worry when we can pray?

Under the everlasting arms of God, we have carried all our children in our bosoms and vision before they were born. We dedicated them to the God of heaven who has been gracious and merciful to us, right in their mother's womb. I have spoken great things to their destinies before and since they were born; I have spiked their destinies with blessings in the best places and palaces in the world, I have spoken excellence into their lives, as I flew across oceans and lands in those parts of the world I visited. I have unleashed the angels that have redeemed me and blessed me into their lives and future; such that no one can curse them.

Together, under the everlasting arms of God, we knelt before the altar of God and dedicated our lives to God and while I laid my hands on them as a priest and as their first pastor. Every day of worship we took Holy Communion together and we dedicate our lives to God with prayer and fasting. I have passed on to them the 'generational' blessings that have followed me. Therefore, our children are unstoppable in their advances into victory.

A word of comfort here. All our fathers of faith were buried with full honor, amid their children despite their struggles and troubles. Even David, with blood in his hands died with a wise and prosperous son on his throne. So, cheer up and don't give up concerning the situation of your children. The Lord our God is our great reward.

CHAPTER 10
MY TEACHING ADVENTURES

I fell in love with teaching and writing very early in life and God has been gracious to me by giving me great opportunities to 'flex' my teaching muscle. Even though working in the oil industry was very attractive, financially, I went for graduate degrees to satisfy my hunger for impacting knowledge. After a PhD, degree in Geology, I tried finding a teaching job but instead landed a research job. I tried to volunteer to teach in the department where I graduated from but was repudiated just because I belonged to an opposing camp in their deadly division. Then I turned to teaching the Bible and biblical concepts to young people in my church. The response to my teaching was powerful and prodigious and my church career spanned three decades. Then God brought me to the United States and provided an excellent teaching career for me.

And God has been good and gracious to me. What I offered to do for gratis in Nigeria without acceptance, has now given me the opportunity of a lifetime to teach the 'entire' world in Colleges and the Universities. The first breakthrough I received on coming to this country was a fellowship and funding for teacher's training by the most prestigious organization in the USA. I then went ahead to devour every book and attended every professional development in teaching. I went from Kindergarten to College to observe how to teach in this completely different civilization. Eventually I became one of the first awardees of a

Certificate of Excellence in teaching Physical Sciences, with endorsement by the American Committee of College and University Educator. I then set my heart to be the best teacher in the world. Not only that I am daily drawing inspiration from the greatest teacher and reminder, Jesus Christ, who is the wisdom of God. Blessed be God forever.

Then I was privileged to volunteer to teach college students on parole as part of my option as a Woodrow Wilson Fellow. To be extremely qualified to pull the positive triggers in people's life I had to go where the greatest Teacher went, the prison. My first day at the prison was a negative and a positive watershed. Before leaving my house, I had palpitations in my heart, based on the picture of prisoners in Nigerian notorious jails. I was expecting prisoners that are filled with dopes who will answer questions with disdain for an African man with an accent teaching earth science. But I had this confidence in my success in teaching at four colleges. Then I met the rudest shocks in my life.

The lady who is about the age of my children oversaw the security scanning machine. He looked at me like a tiger ready to pounce on her prey, and noticed from my body language that I was a stranger to this system. She muttered with deadly finality as I pushed my stuff into the machine' 'if you are not careful here this prison may be your future home'. It was an intelligent insult I was not used to. Apparently, she didn't know I was a professor, and her power drunken state did not allow her to see that I was carrying a glory that cannot be disdained. Here I was, a spiritual and academic 'general' standing before a relatively uneducated and uncouth 'prison warden' being insulted yet smiling. I smiled because I remember a greater General was slapped and disdained and yet he restrained himself. He could have called the armies of heaven to crush such unholy insurrection, but he knew why he was there. I knew why I was sent to the prison to teach to transform their lives, to show by my success story as a scientist that God can rescue, restore and renew anyone.

Reflecting on my tenure as a Woodrow Wilson Teaching Fellow in New Jersey over four enriching years, I'm flooded with nostalgia. Nestled within public schools and jailhouses, amidst a predominantly African American community, I dedicated myself to nurturing brilliance and beauty, not succumbing to stereotypes of savagery or inferiority.

Throughout my teaching journey, I meticulously documented the exceptional achievements of historical and contemporary African American figures. Empirical data, gathered from personal and collaborative research in premier archaeometry laboratories, illuminated the technological prowess of my ancestors. Their innovations, ranging from materials capable of powering rockets to virtually indestructible glass, stand as a testament to their ingenuity despite centuries of adversity.

My writings have celebrated luminaries like Dr. Washington Carver, whose scientific inventions and patents paved the way for progress. I've championed Katherine Johnson, the 'human computer,' whose calculations propelled American spacecraft, and the pioneering Consultant Ophthalmologist whose Laserphaco Probe revolutionized cataract treatment.

Yes, African Americans have faced profound setbacks, but every civilization, from British to Persian to Greek to Jewish, has encountered its own trials. Many have seized upon these challenges as opportunities for monumental leaps forward, shaping brighter futures for generations to come. I firmly believe in the potential for African American science and technology to rise from the ashes of adversity, leaving an indelible mark on the world.

I am resolute in my commitment to utilizing my scientific expertise to uncover African discoveries, reshaping the mindset of young African Americans and their diasporic kin. The resources, indomitable spirit, intellect, and financial means are all within our grasp. What we lack are individuals willing to ignite positive change in our youth, awakening the vast intellectual and creative potential lying dormant within them.

There are not inherently bad or good brains—only untrained and trained brains. Neuroscience reinforces this, echoing the wisdom found in ancient scriptures. Do not allow anyone to sell you the lie that you are inferior because you were made in the image of God, who commands the cosmos and dwells within you.

Through the grace of God, my teaching has been very successful, transcending the borders of the United States, into all the continents of the world. This culminated in my being hired as a Professor at the largest public university, the University of Maryland, Global Campus, with great global reach. Not only do I enjoy the teaching adventures, but through my online teaching in almost all nations of the world, I am also able to go back in time to all the nations I had visited as a researcher and global scientist. All glory be to God who has made me a witness that you can be a scientist and a true man of God at the same time.

CHAPTER 11
HANDLING THE INTERRUPTION IN LIFE

On Thanksgiving Day, I experienced a profound encounter with God, teaching me the art of gratitude even amidst three harrowing, life-threatening challenges. How do we make sense of life's paradoxes? One may endure the surgeon's scalpel yet find renewed vitality, or a prayerful soul may emerge unscathed from a near-fatal accident only to receive unexpected blessings, like a dream car. How does a faithful believer navigate through a devastating physical setback only to be catapulted into a new realm of significance? These are the perplexities I've grappled with in a single year.

I have had several of such interruptions to my life, some of them were so severe, and I never thought I would recover from them. Does that sound familiar to you? Please note this. Most successful people have gone through some terrible failures, such as a financial downturn, a divorce, a spate of sickness, some crash moral failures and so on.

Consider the poignant narrative of a woman once labeled barren, enduring years of shame, only to tragically lose her husband in a drunken accident on New Year's Day. Cast out from her home, she sought refuge in our church, and I prayed for her in the name of the Lord. Through what can only be described as divine intervention, she found love anew and, miraculously, within a year, welcomed twins into the world. Such occurrences defy rational explanation, veiled in mystery. Take a moment to contemplate your own journey. What challenges confront you, and what unexpected blessings might be poised to reveal themselves just beyond the horizon?

Interruptions in life is a vast and interesting concept that resonates throughout the Bible and the contemporary world situations! Every civilization be they British, Persian, Greek or Jewish have gone through at least one interruption. Some were deported for hundreds of years from their homelands. An estimated six million Jews were slaughtered by the Nazis and Africans have been violently uprooted from their homelands, which caused disruptions in their development. Many of these nations have been able to turn these interruptions from being a catastrophic interregnum, to an interface for a destiny leap into a better and more brilliant future for their children. Others remain stagnant and are complaining of injustices thousands of years after the initial unconformity!

As I was teaching my students, incarcerated in the jail, when I received a light from heaven, an inspiration that will transform a geological concept into a revolutionary application to social life. The subject was 'unconformity', a period of loss of geological records because of an interruption or hiatus in sedimentation. I asked my students, some of them serving life sentences, but now qualified for parole. 'What social situations can be regarded as an interruption in life?' One of them answered with a fist, 'Incarceration'! That was what began a new dimension of my teaching 'revelation'.

This indicates that we can determine what we are going to make up from the episodic interruptions in our lives. It's up to us either to translate these seemingly negative occurrences in our lives, into a positive interface, to prepare us for destiny leaps into a new dimension of superabundant living; or we can transfer them to a negative interregnum of depression, despondency and eventually death. This is like placing your car in neutral gear or reverse gear. But the interruption can become an interface to lead us into new breakthroughs or an interregnum permanently damaging our chances of recovery.

But you can unleash the greatest creative force in your life even though you are amid incarceration. That is what I encouraged my students in the jailhouse to do, and many of them graduated in flying colors, were pardoned and are now very successful in their chosen vocations. You can display life even though your living room is surrounded by funeral homes, and you can display health and wealth in the presence of a vicious pandemic and in the precincts of poverty. That was what happened at the grave of Lazarus despite the projections of the Pharisees; it happened when Jesus rose from the dead, despite the deals among the principalities and powers; it has happened to me. You can resurrect and be alive again despite despair and despondency surrounding your destiny. You can celebrate in the solemnity of the cemetery, and you can smile amid severe storms. You too can. Yes, you can, no matter what is going on here. The one who stabilizes the stars and calls them by their names can surely resurrect your dying or decayed life!

CHAPTER 12
ON THE MATCH AGAIN

I believe I was created by a special sovereign act of God; otherwise, I would not have been able to survive the wicked and boisterous challenges that shaped my destiny. There is no logical explanation for how I have lived more than seventy years, marked by mercy and unexplainable successes and breakthroughs. I don't deserve it, nor could I have earned it. God has shown mercy to my lineage.

I have been in a hurry all my life—to get educated, to have children and grandchildren, and even to retire. This urgency stemmed from my tumultuous childhood, marked by illness, satanic attacks, and personal struggles. I never imagined I would make it this far in life. The initial plan was to do everything quickly and wrap up my affairs, as I was not expected to live past seventeen years. Yet, the omnipotent, omniscient, and omnipresent arms of God have carried me through more than seventy successful years. It wasn't until God appeared to me and transformed me into a new, sharp threshing instrument with teeth that I found my true path.

And just as I was thinking my academic and achievement journey of life is winding up, strange words from strange sources came to revive me. I was even thinking of writing my will when God slapped me to my senses and then gave me three matching orders. To intervene by intercession. To write for the transformation of lives and to speak to ignite hope. With such massive orders from God, my Redeemer, I had to go back to the spiritual and physical gyms, to build muscles for the assignment ahead, for the journey is long!

Then COVID came from the blues which confined almost everyone into a corner and crushed any creativity I could muster. In my case I could not go to church for almost two years and my worship was on the TV. This time was also a period of political upheaval in the United States where I live and work. I was studying the spiritual dimension of the struggle for the soul of the nation when I encountered a Messianic Rabbi who was calling the nation to repent as the solution to the malaise. I was glued to his broadcasts, bought almost all his published works and subscribed to all his channels. I literally became his disciple, right in the corner of my living room. And as soon as the churches were opened, I jumped into my car and I became a member of this amazing community of the Jerusalem Centre, in Wayne, New Jersey.

For two years, this Messianic Rabbinical Center served as a Bible College where I rewired my brain and reignited the power of ministry and mysteries in God. The pains of the past disappeared, my cynicism about life was crushed, and the spiritual energy necessary for my life to shine with brilliance was released into every fiber of my being. God then ignited my original gift of prayer and transformed me into a 'praying mantis'. He sharpened my ability to speak in tongues and endowed me with the gift of a ready writer, infusing new energy into my life. Since then, I have never been the same again.

Then there were over four credible prophecies supporting this new vision. Firstly, during an anointing service at a church meeting I attended, a pastor prophesied that God had commanded me to write 'large books that will transform a generation'. Secondly, during a teaching engagement with prisoners, a mysterious voice spoke to me, affirming that God intended to make me great again. Thirdly, upon returning home that day, I received an email prophecy from a stranger in Australia confirming these words. These four credible sources, without contradiction, included Dr. Mrs. Agbaje, the editor of this book, who offered her assistance 'gratis' when I asked for it.

The pinnacle of God's revelation for my future arrived on Sunday, June 3, 2023, just days after my sixty-ninth birthday. In an unexpected encounter, an old, bearded man playing music at the Jerusalem Center met me in the bathroom and delivered a prophecy. He proclaimed that God is bringing greater glory into my life. That same year, I faced three near-death experiences—an accident, a severe fall, and a surgical intervention. Yet, it was also a year of significant successes and miracles. Such a mighty God, such a merciful Savior, such a wonder-working God, has shown me favors I never deserved and could not have earned.

God also reminded me of his mysterious dealing in my life so far. The story was like this. When God saw that my enemies were surrounding me and would have derailed my destiny, He stopped the world to get me out of my country because of His mercies and love. There were two options opened for God: either for Him to translate me to heaven or transfer me out of the reach of my adversaries. He decided, in His mercies to choose the latter option.

The story goes like this. More than ten million people from all corners of the world balloted for 50 thousand visas under the USA diversity visa. The computer picked the required number of people by the middle of the year, and they started the process of immigration. Then God took me to the USA for the first time in my life. I went to deliver a lecture on my landmark discovery of ancient glass making tradition in south-western Nigeria. As I was about to board the aircraft back to Nigeria, God spoke to me to prophesy to the gates of America to open to me. I did as it was commanded.

Immediately I returned to Nigeria; the government of the United States discovered a computer error in that year's selection for the immigrants in that category and decided to cancel the entire selection from all over the world. This evoked a legal battle by those who were already selected. It went up to the supreme courts where the US government's position was upheld, and the initial selection was canceled.

Then the US government reprogrammed their selection, and I was among the winners. Recently God explained to me what happened. He said He stopped the world for a space of three months because of the words I spoke when I was leaving the USA. The Spirit of God gathered the words and placed them in my mouth. His mighty arms then performed the words. God had done this before when Joshua gave similar commands and the Sun stood still for the space of one day. Why will God stop the whole world because of one man; why will God stop the sun from going down because of one man. He did the impossible when Elisa's dead bones raised a dead man that encountered it, when the blind received their sights, when the barren received power to conceive and when our Lord Jesus went to the cross to crush all curses that were pursuing us.

That is the message I have for everyone reading this book. You cannot navigate the roads of life with knowledge and skills alone. Having earned my PhD over three decades ago, I have taught thousands of students across the world and traveled to almost all the great nations of the world. I can testify to the existence of a God who can make you great. He is the source of greatness for everyone; He brings one down and lifts another up. He is the God of Abraham, Isaac, and the father of our Lord Jesus. The other gods are cold, capricious, cosmic nothingness.

I invite you to come under the canopy of His mighty wings today and enter into the commonwealth of Israel and the Covenant of hope in Christ Jesus. Jesus is the reason for your living. I am a witness that God works perfectly, no matter what is happening in the world, how boisterous the billows are, or how wicked the whirlwinds may appear.

I will therefore encourage you to put this book down, bow before your Creator in full surrender and give your life to Jesus Christ, the only one whose Blood atones for our sins however messy and unclean we are. It's that simple. I did that more than thirty years back and the journey is sweeter still. And I have dedicated the rest of my life to telling the stories of God's goodness to me and His faithfulness that never fails.

ABOUT THE AUTHOR

Akin Ige, PhD, was a Professor of Geology for several years in Nigeria and also served as a priest in both the Church of Nigeria and the United States. Over the years, he has received numerous prestigious awards from around the world, including three honors from the Royal Society. He is currently a Professor of Astronomy, Geology, and Environmental Science in the United States.

From a young age, Akin faced formidable challenges—forces that sought to alter his destiny even before birth. Yet, his life stands as a testament to God's grace, a grace that has empowered him to touch countless lives through his prayer and deliverance ministry for more than three decades. His journey is nothing short of miraculous. He has always believed that his existence is the result of a "Sovereign Act" of God—an intervention so profound that it not only allowed him to survive the dangers of his childhood but also to thrive against overwhelming odds. The storms around him were fierce and perilous, yet by God's grace, he was spared.

In gratitude for reaching the milestone of seventy years, he now shares the spiritual principles that have sustained him and guided his success in life and ministry.

This book serves as a download of heavenly wisdom designed to transform the lives of God's sons and daughters. It seeks to break the chains of evil forces and spiritual stagnation, helping individuals shine like the stars they were destined to be. It aims to unleash their vast intellectual and spiritual potential, propelling them toward the superabundant life that was designed for them long before their birth.

APPENDIX - TRIBUTES

A Tribute On The Platinum Celebration Of An Iconic Personality

It gives me great joy to celebrate the Platinum Birthday Anniversary of an illustrious Ven. Professor Olugbenga Ige. He is a distinguished scholar of international repute with ripple positive impacts.

I have known Prof. Ige, for more than two decades and we became closer in relationship when him and his team played the unique roles in facilitating my appointment as the full-time Assistant Chaplain of All Soul's Chapel, Obafemi Awolowo University, Ile-Ife, Osun State Nigeria, in the year 2011.

On the occasion of attaining this special milestone, it gladdens our hearts to celebrate and attest to the character of such an iconic personality, which is a true embodiment of excellence, faith, and love. Your unwavering dedication to serving God as a fearless preacher and teacher of God's Word is reflected in your life and lips. Also, your profound knowledge of the Word of God as an erudite scholar and your role as a consummate family man exemplify true greatness.

Succinctly, your unwavering patriotism, your loyalty, and your dedication to your native land are qualities that inspire us all.
Sir, on this momentous occasion of your Platinum celebration, it is our sincere prayer that you will continue to shine brightly like a diamond, illuminating the lives of those around you with your wisdom, kindness, and grace.

May your journey ahead be filled with abundant blessings, good health, and joyous moments surrounded by loved ones with divine flourishing like the palm tree as you age graciously in Him. Amen.

Again, as you reflect on the meaningful journey of your life at seventy, as the beloved of God, may you be filled with a sense of accomplishment and fulfilment, as the Almighty God brings you into the fullness of your inheritance and perfects all that concerns you and your family in Jesus name.

Your legacy will forever be etched in the hearts of those who have had the privilege of knowing you like me, whom you gave a veritable platform for service to God and humanity.

This comes with every blessing in Him.
Sola Gratia

The Rt. Rev'd. Stephen Adeniran Oni, Ph.D(Ib.), Mcasson, FAT
Lord Bishop, Diocese of Ondo

Tributes To Papa Ige

Thanks dad for the foundation you have laid for me in everything, in fact in every aspect of my life. I take time to pause to ruminate on the principles I have seen you apply in your own life, and it has worked for me quite well

This time I just want to appreciate God in you specifically in the aspect of marriage, ministry and home building.

Many things people seek literature and prayer to learn have been given to me practically from God through the life that both of you have lived in my presence. This cuts across so many fields in married life, from financial management, to how to live peaceably with one another, how to deal with In-laws and the influence of the extended family and very importantly raising children. Both of you may not give me a billion dollars in cash but you have given me much more. You have given me a Godly culture that my generation will learn from.

You know that when a man reads something and gets insight from it, it becomes a revelation to him and when he practices it then it becomes a Law to him and his family.

The beauty of the life I have seen you live is that many of the things you have taught me have become laws to me for my future and I don't need to read about some things again because I have seen them work for you. As a matter of fact, each time I read about some principles of life, some do not sound new to me because I have seen it being practiced. Your actions by the grace of God had promoted me from the stage of seeking and revelation to that of Law in some aspects of my life and ministry.

I must thank and appreciate you but the best way I can to say this is to improve more on this Godly culture and pass it on to the next generation by practically giving myself wholly to it.

Your Son,
Daniel Ige

To My Father @70

Your unwavering dedication to prayer has shaped my life profoundly. Each morning, you prayed for me, instilling in me the importance of sanctifying the day before it begins. I am not the only beneficiary, you inspired my friend who was quietly watching, and who now prays for his daughter every morning.

From you I have learned of the power of persistence before God and man through numerous life examples where you have refused to give up on life, your dreams and your children.

Thank you for your inspiration,
David Ige

Tribute Daddy Ige @70

Daddy, what a beautiful blessing you are to us all! Your faith, your joy, your generosity, and your love—every bit of you—is a true example of Christ Himself. Thank you for choosing to live life according to His Word. How easy it is to celebrate you and what an honor it is to know you. We declare by faith that this will be your best year yet!
Thank you for your exemplary life. Thank you for shining light upon us all. Thank you for the Spirit of patience and understanding. We are forever blessed to have encountered you. Even in this season, God will cause you to do more exploits in Jesus' name. Happy 70th birthday sir!

Engineer Pastor Muyiwa Ojo

Tribute To A Worthy And Quintessential Ambassador Ven. Prof. Olugbenga Akin Ige

Happy 70th birthday to my esteemed Daddy, mentor, and inspiration, Ven. Prof. Akin Ige!

Seven decades of life, wisdom, and impact. Your journey has been a blessing to our Family, Academia, and the world at large. From my primary school days to date, you have been a constant guide, mentor, and role model. Your wisdom, patience, and encouragement have shaped me into the person I am today.

Your dedication to education, research, and community service is a testament to your selflessness and commitment to excellence. You have inspired generations of students, colleagues, and family members, including me through your wonderful daily morning prayers which have never ceased for almost 10 years till date, what a wonderful inspiration!

As you celebrate this milestone, I celebrate you - your life, legacy, and unwavering support. May this new chapter bring you continued joy, good health, and fulfillment in Jesus' name

Thank you for being an extraordinary Daddy and mentor. I love you, and I wish you a happy 70th birthday!

ESV Olasunkoye Joel Adelowo ANIVS, RSV
Principal Partner, Olasunkoye & Co, Estate Surveyors and Valuers, ABUJA, Nigeria

---

Tribute To Daddy Ige @70

I have known Prof. Akin Ige for 36 years, having met him when I was a young teenager. He disciplined us youths and taught us life skills using biblical principles. His drive and commitment to ensuring our success are unparalleled. Prof. Ige is a knowledgeable, intelligent, and highly practical professor with outstanding mentoring skills. I am proud to say he played a crucial role in my achievements as a family man and as a Global Director of Engineering in a Fortune 500 company.

Your foresight is unmatched. I remember you preaching from the pulpit, sharing with us the importance of seizing job opportunities abroad, even in places like Saudi Arabia. From that lesson, I learned that we have the God-given ability to explore the world and be our best. In 2018, during a phone conversation, you shared another valuable lesson with me: sometimes, we must stoop to conquer. You supported this with biblical examples, and that message came at a perfect time for me. It emphasized the importance of humility in achieving success, and I continue to share this wisdom with my loved ones, friends, associates, and colleagues.

Akintoye Akinyoade MS (ISU), EMBA (KSU)
Global Director of Engineering
Owens Corning USA

Tribute Professor Akin Ige @70

It is a privilege for me to address you as I did when we were young. You are not just my only blood brother, but a pillar of strength and love in my life. From the earliest days, you protected me fiercely, ensuring no harm befell me. Your guidance and unwavering support have been instrumental in shaping my life's journey and achieving all that I have accomplished. Your love for me surpasses even that of our father, extending generously to my wife and children. Your encouragement, prayers, and financial support for my family have been exceptional, and I am forever grateful.

You have graciously welcomed me into your family, where your wife exemplifies faithfulness, love, and virtue, and your children reflect the values you both uphold. It is evident that God has blessed your home abundantly.

As we celebrate your 70th birthday, I am overwhelmed with gratitude for the profound bond we share. From childhood adventures to facing life's trials as adults, you have consistently been my rock, offering guidance, support, and inspiration. Your kindness, empathy, and generosity have touched countless lives, including mine. Your passion for the gospel, counseling, and prayer is infectious, and your sense of humor has brightened many of our days.

I am immensely proud of your achievements, especially becoming the first professor and Archdeacon in the Church of Nigeria, Anglican Communion, a milestone unparalleled in our lineage and upbringing. Your dedication and perseverance are a testament to your character and faith. As you reach this significant milestone, I wish you continued health, happiness, and fulfillment. May your life be perpetually blessed with love, laughter, and purpose.

Thank you for being not just an incredible brother but a role model beyond comparison. Words cannot express how much I love you. Happy 70th birthday, dear brother.

With all my love,
Your only blood brother
Revd. Olufemi Ige

Ven Professor O Akin Ige @70

It took me a long time before I could write this. I consider myself extremely fortunate to have Ven. Prof. Akin Ige as a mentor in the Christian faith and the Anglican Ministry.

I first had direct contact with you when you were invited to minister at the first anniversary of the Anglican Youth Fellowship at St. Andrew Anglican Church, Oke Amola, Modakeke, in 1990 (then in the Diocese of Ibadan). I was a member of the planning committee.

Later, as the president of the Anglican Youth Fellowship Modakeke, I had the opportunity to work closely with you as our Youth Chaplain for many years. In 1999, you invited me to join you at All Saints Anglican Church as a minister, where we worked together. You pastored the church for fourteen solid years, transforming it from a sitting room to a big auditorium, the Sanctuary of Solution. I was able to tap into some of your anointing and impartations.

I am also grateful to you as a mentor, for your tutelage and encouragement in the Anglican Ministry as a frontliner. You are a rugged evangelist and prayer warrior who believes in faith and action. You are an evangelical strategist who is always surrounded by people and is also sympathetic to the cause of the less privileged in the church and academic world. In everything, you are blunt, honest, and forthright, making it easy to use your resources for good works and evangelism.

You possess the faith of Abraham, the spirit of prayer and praise like David, and the unconditional love of Joseph. You have led many to Christ, including my father, the late Pa Joseph Olanrewaju Adigun. It was mentioned in my father's biography that Ven. Ige said we should surrender everything and belong to Jesus.

I cannot forget you in my life, for you promoted my ministerial assignment and boosted my career through your connections. I cannot forget your passion during the time I was writing my first-degree project. When I could no longer find a way forward, you linked me up with professors of Mathematics at Obafemi Awolowo University, which enhanced my distinction in the project. Your message on the day of our wedding as a preacher still lingers.

As a frontliner in evangelism in our diocese, it took me a long time to adjust when you relocated to the United States of America. I still carry you along in my ministerial stages today for prayers and words of advice, which have kept me going.

"Baba, as you are celebrating your 70th birthday, although the Psalm says that the days of our years are 70 years, that was in the Old Testament. By the covenant of longevity of life through Jesus Christ, you will live long to accomplish those things that God has for you. The Lord will renew your strength like the eagle and bless your new age. May your birthday be like the start of a year filled with new opportunities, accomplishments, and endless joy."

Rev Canon and Mrs Omokehinde Adigun

To my Second Daddy, Pastor, Lecturer and Mentor, Ven Professor Akin Ige@70

Special days belong to special people with special personalities and are celebrated specially by special people that know the meaning of specialty and the importance of being special, you are special to me and that is why you deserve this special tribute on this occasion of your special day to celebrate your milestone birthday anniversary.

On this special occasion of your 70th birthday anniversary, with my heart full of gratitude and happiness to celebrate a special man who has dedicated his life to the service of GOD, the source of hope to many youths like me and the betterment of youths particularly. I want to specially extend my heartfelt gratitude for your unwavering dedication to GOD's work, boundless love, inspiring guidance and compassionate leadership that my siblings and I have benefited from through many years growing up.

For decades, you have been a source of wisdom, a beacon of hope through your teachings (for me as my Pastor and Lecturer), and a steadfast shepherd guiding your flock with love. Your commitment to nurturing my faith has touched countless lives, your teachings/sermons have inspired me, your counsels have brought relieve in so many situations, and your exemplary life has shown me the true meaning of how to live a life of JESUS CHRIST. Your kindness and generosity know no bounds, whether through a simple smile, a warm hug or a thoughtful prayer, you showed me what it means to truly lift up the spirit of people around me and to love my neighbors the way I love myself.

Thank you for being a guiding light in my journey of life, I thank GOD for the gift of you and for the light you bring into many lives you have touched. May your days be filled with joy, your heart with peace, and your spirit with the unwavering faith that has been the cornerstone of your ministry.

I look forward to the many more years of wisdom and guidance in good health and sound mind. Happy 70th Birthday Anniversary Daddy!!! I am lucky and blessed to have you in my life.

With love, Akin Egbebi
(Your Soldier of CHRIST)

Tribute To A Father And Mentor The Venerable Professor Akin Ige

It is my utmost pleasure to write this tribute to him while he is alive and in celebration of his 70th birthday. I met Venerable around 2008, when I was a teenager, he was the pioneer Dean of our Cathedral of St Stephen, Itaasin Modakeke, Nigeria. An astute scholar and indefatigable preacher, he made me love Anglicanism and I am eternally grateful to have met him at that time of my life when it was scarce to find a model around. He is a godly example of those who Apostle Paul talks about in Hebrews 6:12

In 2013, when I was seeking admission to study Medicine in the Obafemi Awolowo University Ile-Ife Nigeria, my Vicar, Ven 'Debo Babalola took me to Ven. Prof. Akin Ige in the latter's office at the Natural History Museum on the University campus. Prof Akin Ige threw his weight around me and even though I didn't get admission into Clinical Sciences, I entered White House Chemistry. That was the last time I heard from Prof for almost 2 years until 2015, because he left the country just a few days after giving me reference letters.

The following year, in 2014, I got admission to study Medicine and Surgery in the prestigious Premier University in Nigeria; the University of Ibadan. In April 2015, after resumption into 100 level, I sent an email to Prof requesting an audience to tell him about my career and life journey, and despite him being abroad, and with a very busy schedule, we talked on phone for about two hours. I am very grateful for all the advice, support and encouragement he gave me on my journey.

Even though I knew since 2013 that I am going to be a minister of the Gospel, I could not fathom the clarity as at then as all my focus was to become a Surgeon and a Kingdom financier and not a Pastor. But as I continued my walk with God, I began to see clearly the path that God ordained for me and when I needed counsel about Anglican ministry, I contacted Prof and I am thankful to God through him, for the wise counsel and admonition.

On this occasion of your 70th Birthday, Daddy, I pray that God in His mercies grant you sound mind and perfect health to enjoy all the fruits of your labor. May your strength be renewed like eagles, and may you enjoy fulfillment in your old age.
My regards to Mummy and the family.

Your son,
Rev'd Dr. Abiodun D. Akintayo,
MB;BS (Ib), BTh (CGTS),
Curate at Victory Anglican Church, Southampton UK.

Celebrating Prof Akin Ige's 70th Birthday: A Life Of Learning, Service And Love

Today, we gather to celebrate a man who has worn many hats throughout his life, each with the same unwavering dedication and grace: Dad, Professor, and Reverend Akin Ige.

For Seven decades, Prof Akin Ige has enriched the lives of countless people of which I am proud to be among them. As a father, his love and guidance has been a source of strength and support. He's instilled in us valuable lessons that go beyond textbooks -lessons about compassion, hard work, integrity, faith, prayer and the importance of always striving to learn and grow.

Professor Akin Ige's passion for knowledge is contagious. He has inspired countless students with his insightful lectures and dedication to their academic pursuit. His contributions to the field of Geology are a testament to his intellectual curiosity and commitment to furthering knowledge.

As clergyman, his faith has been a guiding light not only for himself but for everyone he encounters. His sermon, and prayers he sends every morning to us resonate with wisdom and compassion, offering comfort and inspiration to those in need.

But beyond these titles, Dad Prof Akin Ige is simply a remarkable human being. His warmth, humor and gentle spirit are qualities that everyone who knows his cherishes. He has a gift for making everyone feel valuable and seen, always offering a listening ear.

Seventy years is a milestone but feels more like the beginning of a new character. I am incredibly grateful for the impact Prof has had on my life and others. I look forward to many more years of learning from his wisdom, basking in his love and celebrating his incredible journey.

HAPPY 70th BIRTHDAY SIR
Deacon Dayo ADEPOJU (Osun State Nigeria)

Tribute Professor Akin Ige @70

Congratulations on your 70th birthday anniversary! Your profound impact on the church, academia, and humanity at large is truly remarkable. Your messages through books, social media, the pulpit, and your prayers resonate deeply and will continue to inspire both now and for generations to come. We are grateful to have crossed paths with a man of such immense blessing and influence. May you continue to thrive in health and vitality as you further the work of His kingdom.

With heartfelt joy, we celebrate this milestone with you and pray that the Lord blesses your new age abundantly in Jesus' name.

Rev and Mrs Debo Adeyemo

Tribute to Prof. Akin Ige @70

You're my hero! I have known Professor Akin Ige for 28 years and since then I have asked him for help and he's always willing to drop everything to lend a hand. He's the rock of stability in my family. My son shares his first and middle name.

In my educational stream, he boosted my motivation level and facilitated my coming to America for my doctoral program. He's a supportive mentor who inspired me to my best version. He never imposed his opinion on me and has always respected my viewpoint. His kindness, support, and interest in my life and career have helped me in many difficult stages of my life.

I am humbled by the challenge of describing the fullness of God's grace upon his life. Prof. Akin Ige made a difference in the lives of hundreds of students at Obafemi Awolowo University, and the congregation at All Saints' church for years, and his kindness and positivity left an unwavering legacy in the communities.
Thank you for calling me your sister and being our spiritual father - my best wishes for this next chapter in your life.

Taiwo Bamidele

Tribute to Prof. Akinlolu Ige

I am highly pleased to write a tribute for my father in the Lord within the Anglican Communion and my senior colleague at the Natural History Museum of Obafemi Awolowo University, Nigeria. Professor Akinlolu Ige has been a mentor and missionary to my life and to the church at large. The best and most beautiful things in this world cannot be seen or even touched; we only feel them in our hearts. This latest Septuagenarian has been a bridge that makes these beautiful things felt and touched in my life. He shows love and passion, driving me to the land of fulfillment. He is not just a father in the Lord to me but a very zealous man who will not let you rest until you do the right thing.

Permit me to call him "Dean," another name he acquired in Ife East Diocese Anglican Communion, Nigeria, during his service in the vineyard of our Lord Jesus Christ. Before his relocation to the USA, Dean was our German machine in Evangelism. He had occupied the post I currently hold as Diocesan Evangelism coordinator. He would distribute money and clothing to people during village evangelism. The money he used to buy the clothing was sourced outside church funds; he would find money for us and even add his own to do charity during evangelism. Dean Ige has bought us different motorcycles for evangelism in our Diocese, which I believe he will continue to help us acquire more for evangelism at his 70th birthday. He made himself available during evangelism, physically following us on motorcycles to all the villages that are not easily accessible by car. He is a man that you can easily approach and consult any time and day. He is not selfish or self-centered when dealing with people within and outside the church environment.

It is also pertinent to mention in this tribute that the most beautiful edifice building at Obafemi Awolowo University, known as the Museum building, was achieved during Professor Akinlolu Ige's tenure as our then Director. The zeal and commitment of this industrious researcher, teacher and communicator, helped him achieve this unprecedented success. This world-award-winning building had been abandoned for about three decades before Professor Ige became our Director. He easily and readily works with his colleagues, and he understands team spirit very well.

Professor Akin Ige we are proud of you in Obafemi Awolowo University at large. Keep the ball rolling as you join your mates in septuagenarian group.

Dr. Oyeseyi Joshua OYELADE,
Senior lecturer at Obafemi Awolowo University, Nigeria
Evangelist in Ife East Anglican communion (Church of Nigeria).

Tribute to my friend @70

I have known Rev. (Dr.) Akin Ige for almost 40 years during our time together at the Hospital Christian Fellowship, which has grown to become Christ Way Ministries International in Ile-Ife, Osun State. Nigeria. We were part of the Faith Clinic, Prayer and Evangelism team of the ministry. We were also colleagues at the University Of Ife, now Obafemi Awolowo University in Ile-Ife.

I can testify that Rev. Ige is a strong prayer warrior, dedicated, and a faithful minister of the Gospel as we traveled together around Osun State in those days.

After leaving Christ Way Ministries, he continued his ministerial work by starting and pastoring churches within the Anglican Communion in Ile-Ife while maintaining a full-time position at the university. Even today, he continues with his prayer ministry and provides daily prayer mandates to the body of Christ.

Furthermore, Dr. Ige is an active scholarly researcher with several publications to his credit. He helped to secure grants and expanded the work and collections of the Natural History Museum at the Obafemi Awolowo University during his tenure as a Professor and Head of the Natural History Museum at the University.

Thus, it is refreshing to see that Rev. (Dr.) Akin Ige has decided to write his autobiography to encourage and share his experiences in the ministry, journey of his faith as a disciple of Jesus Christ and academic life with the world. This is indeed a noble endeavor that will encourage others now and many generations to come.

This is a must-read for Christian scholars. This body of work clearly shows that you can pursue academics and be fully committed to the Christian faith as a disciple of Jesus Christ.

Thanks to my brother for this marvelous scholarly work.
We pray that God will continue to bless and fill you with His presence, more fresh anointing, and more wisdom to serve God faithfully to the very end.

Rev Dr Ikoba

Thank you for your love, kindness and prayers – Happy 70th birthday

Celebrating our 23rd wedding anniversary, and recently my wife's 60th birthday, I've been reflecting on the cherished memories we've shared with you over the years. My appreciation is deed, for the affection, friendship, the laughter, and the experiences we lived through as we grew. You have been a part of our journey in a special way, and we hold dear the bond we created. I want to say thank you for the kind of love you've shown to our family.

My wife and I wish you the best as you celebrate your 70th birthday. Over the years, we have seen you do so many things to make life full of smiles and love. We appreciate you for every wonderful memory that we have created together, and for the roles you played in it. We've been through thick and thin, and you stood with us. I remember when we were waiting for children, your visit, prayer and encouragement was amazing. It is simply your nature and lifestyle to do something to put smiles on other people's faces. We celebrate you. God has made you a source of blessing and you are blessed.

To encourage and strengthen us, you freely shared many stories of difficult situations and tough challenges that God made you to overcome, right from your childhood, youthful life and social background. Now, at 70, here you are – Father, Grand-father, professor with international honours, Canon in the Church of God, an astute academician, a meticulous administrator, a remarkable mentor, and much more… Furthermost, a son of the Most High God. WOW!

If someone asked you when you were 10 years old, if you had any inclination that from such paltry beginnings you could attain such heights as you are at today, your answer will most likely be a hearty laugh saying never in your wildest dreams.

In you I have seen how diligence, hard work, fairness, forthrightness and compassion, with a spirit of excellence has worked, and taken you higher. And with all these, you put on deep and true humility as you unendingly bless and thank God for the waves of miracles and blessings that you have experienced and keep experiencing.

Over the years I've been amazed at your brilliant mastery of self-reinvention; how effortlessly and gracefully you do it with your usual stamp of excellence. At 70, you remain vibrant and relevant not just to me or our family but to an army of people all over the globe. It has been and is always my delight to have a man with your wealth of experience and accomplishments, with a humble soul, bold, bursting charisma and charm, with contagious joyful spirit and a lion heart gushing with such pure unbridled love. At this important landmark in your life, all of us in my family celebrate you now and always....

Happy birthday!
With lots of love,
Dr Joseph BAMIDELE & Dr (Mrs) Omosolape BAMIDELE

Printed in Great Britain
by Amazon

58075135R00046